I0406825

How I Will Make You Rich

By Christian Brewster

A Simple Guide For You To Make More Money

About the author

Christian Brewster has 13 years of experience in entrepreneurship and financial advising, and after his bestselling first book *''BECOME A CMO: How to Attract, Convert and Serve High-Paying Clients*

On Your Terms by being a fractional CMO'' he presents his new book *''How I Will Make You Rich - A Simple Guide For You To Make More Money''*. Christian is an excellent speaker with an incredible story. He has traveled all over the world from Kenya to Dubai and from Europe to America speaking about marketing, advertising, and entrepreneurship. Christian explains what it takes for a person like him who started out working for free as an intern at Ogilvy & Mather before becoming one of their youngest Directors of Business Development ever at only 24 years old.

First Edition Copyright © 2023 Christian Brewster
Written by Christian Brewster

Table Of Contents

Foreword

Welcome! Are you ready to unlock the secrets of wealth and abundance? If you're tired of living paycheck to paycheck, dreaming about that luxurious lifestyle, then this blog post is your golden ticket. Today, I'm going to share with you a simple guide on how to make more money and pave your way toward financial independence.

Picture this: sipping margaritas on a pristine beach, driving luxury cars without batting an eye at the price tag, and enjoying lavish vacations whenever your heart desires. Sound too good to be true? Well, buckle up because I'm about to show you how it's possible! With proven strategies for 2022 and beyond, we'll explore promising ways for you to make money in the coming years.

Introduction

If you've ever wondered how to make your money work for you and transform your financial situation, this book is for you. In this comprehensive guide, you will discover the secrets of building wealth and becoming rich.

The book provides practical strategies and techniques to help you make more money and create a solid financial foundation. From understanding the importance of saving and budgeting to exploring different investment options, this guide covers it all.

You will learn how to develop a money mindset that empowers you to take control of your finances. The book also dives into the world of passive income, teaching you how to generate additional streams of income and make your money work for you even while you sleep.

With step-by-step instructions and real-life examples, this guide will empower you to take charge of your financial future. Whether you are just starting on your financial journey or looking to take your wealth-building efforts to the next level, this book is a valuable resource that will provide the knowledge and inspiration you need.

Don't settle for an average financial situation. Take the first step towards achieving financial freedom by diving into the secrets of building wealth and becoming rich outlined in this book. Your journey to extraordinary financial success starts here.

In today's fast-paced world, financial stability and the pursuit of increased income are top priorities for many individuals. It is crucial to explore different avenues that can help us achieve our financial goals and secure a prosperous future.

One option is to seek higher-paying jobs or career advancements. By continuously improving our skills and knowledge, we can position ourselves for better opportunities and higher income potential. This may involve further education, professional development courses, or networking to expand our connections in our desired industry.

Another avenue to consider is engaging in side hustles or additional streams of income. With the rise of the gig economy and digital platforms, there are numerous opportunities to monetize our skills or hobbies. Whether it's freelancing, starting an online business, or investing in real estate, the possibilities are vast.

It's also important to have a solid financial plan in place. This includes budgeting, saving, and investing wisely. By managing our expenses effectively, setting financial goals, and making informed investment decisions, we can build wealth and secure a prosperous future.

Ultimately, taking action and being proactive in exploring various income-generating opportunities is key. It requires determination, resilience, and a willingness to step out of our comfort zones. With the right mindset and strategic planning, we can increase our income and work towards achieving financial stability in today's competitive world.

Now, before we dive into the practical tips on how to build wealth effectively, let's quickly assess your current financial status. Are you content with your earnings or do you aspire for more? Understanding where you stand financially will provide a solid foundation upon which we can build strategies tailored specifically for you.

Get ready for an exciting journey toward financial abundance! In this comprehensive guide, we will unveil tried-and-true techniques that have helped individuals amass their fortunes. By implementing these strategies, you can increase your income, venture into business ventures, budget wisely, and invest strategically.

One of the key aspects we will explore is diversifying your income streams. By expanding beyond a single source of income, you can create resilience and opportunities for growth. We'll delve into various side hustles, entrepreneurship, or investment options that can help you generate additional revenue.

Budgeting wisely is another crucial element in building wealth. We will provide practical tips on how to track your expenses, prioritize savings, and optimize your spending habits. By managing your money effectively, you can allocate resources toward achieving your financial goals.

Investing strategically is a powerful way to grow your wealth. Whether it's investing in stocks, real estate, or other financial instruments, we will guide you through the principles of investing and help you make informed decisions that align with your risk tolerance and long-term objectives.

Throughout this journey, we will provide step-by-step instructions, actionable advice, and real-life examples to inspire and empower you on your path to financial abundance.

So buckle up and get ready to embark on this transformative journey together. By implementing these proven techniques, you can pave the way toward building wealth and achieving the financial success you aspire to. Let's dive in and unlock your full financial potential!

Assessing Your Wealth: A Quick Take

Assessing your wealth requires a holistic evaluation of your financial situation. Here are some key aspects to consider:

- Income: Take a close look at your income sources, including your primary job, side hustles, investments, and any other sources of revenue. Evaluate the stability and growth potential of each income stream.

- Expenses: Analyze your expenses to understand where your money is going. Categorize your spending into essential (e.g., housing, utilities, food) and discretionary (e.g., entertainment, dining out). This will help you identify areas where you can potentially reduce expenses and save more.

- Assets: Identify and assess your assets, including cash, savings accounts, investments, properties, and other valuable possessions. Calculate their current value and consider their potential for appreciation over time.

- Liabilities: Evaluate your debts, such as mortgages, loans, credit card balances, and any other outstanding obligations. Determine the interest rates, repayment terms, and prioritize paying off high-interest debts.

- Net Worth: Calculate your net worth by subtracting your liabilities from your assets. This provides a snapshot of your overall financial position and helps track your progress over time.

- Financial Goals: Set clear and achievable financial goals that align with your long-term aspirations. These goals can include saving for retirement, building an emergency fund, paying off debts, or investing in specific ventures.

By objectively assessing these aspects, you can gain a comprehensive understanding of your financial situation. This knowledge will serve as the foundation for making informed decisions and developing effective strategies to build and grow your wealth.

It's important to regularly evaluate whether you are earning fair compensation for your skills and expertise. If you feel that your current income does not align with your value in the job market, there are several steps you can take:

- Research Salary Data: Look up industry standards and salary ranges for positions similar to yours.   This will give you a benchmark to compare your current income to.

- Assess Your Value: Evaluate your skills, experience, and expertise. Consider any additional qualifications or certifications you have obtained. Assess how your contributions positively impact your organization.

- Explore Higher-Paying Job Opportunities: Keep an eye out for job openings in your field that offer higher salaries. Update your resume and explore networking opportunities to increase your chances of landing a better-paying role.

- Negotiate: When seeking a new job or during performance reviews, be prepared to negotiate your salary. Highlight your accomplishments, skills, and the value you bring to the position. Research effective negotiation techniques to maximize your chances of success.

- Invest in Education or Certifications: Consider pursuing additional education or certifications to enhance your skills and make yourself more marketable. This can open doors to higher-paying job opportunities or promotions within your current organization.

- Develop a Side Hustle: Explore ways to generate additional income outside of your primary job. This could involve freelancing, consulting, or starting a small business based on your skills and passions.

Increasing your earning potential may require effort and patience. It's important to continuously invest in your personal and professional development and seize opportunities that can lead to higher compensation.

Evaluating your expenses and creating a budget is a crucial step in building wealth. Here's how you can start:

- Track Your Expenses: Begin by tracking all your expenses for a month or two. This will give you a clear picture of where your money is going and help identify areas where you can cut back.

- Categorize Your Expenses: Sort your expenses into categories such as housing, transportation, utilities, groceries, entertainment, and discretionary spending. This will make it easier to analyze and prioritize your spending.

- Identify Unnecessary Expenditures: Review each category and identify expenses that may not be essential or align with your financial goals. These could include dining out frequently, subscription services you don't fully utilize, or impulse purchases.

- Set Spending Limits: Once you've identified unnecessary expenditures, set spending limits for each category. Determine how much you are willing to allocate towards each expense and stick to those limits.

- Prioritize Saving: Make saving a priority in your budget. Set aside a portion of your income for savings and treat it as a non-negotiable expense. Automate your savings by setting up automatic transfers to a separate savings account.

- Find Ways to Reduce Costs: Look for opportunities to cut back on expenses without sacrificing too much. This could involve negotiating bills, shopping for better deals, or finding cost-effective alternatives to certain products or services.

- Regularly Review and Adjust: Revisit your budget periodically to ensure it remains aligned with your financial goals and lifestyle. Adjust your spending limits as needed and celebrate milestones when you achieve your savings targets.

By creating a budget and consciously managing your expenses, you can identify areas where you can cut back without sacrificing too much. Redirecting those funds towards savings and investments will accelerate your journey towards building wealth.

Now turn your attention to the assets that contribute to your net worth. Do you own any valuable investments such as stocks, bonds, or real estate properties? Assess their performance and determine if they align with your long-term financial goals.

On the flip side, don't forget about liabilities – debts that impede wealth accumulation. Paying off high-interest debt should be prioritized as it frees up more money for savings and investing in income-generating opportunities.

Managing and reducing liabilities is crucial for wealth accumulation. Here are some steps you can take to address your debts:

- Create a Debt Inventory: Make a list of all your debts, including credit card balances, student loans, car loans, and any other outstanding loans. Include the total amount owed, interest rates, and minimum monthly payments for each debt.

- Prioritize High-Interest Debts: Identify the debts with the highest interest rates, as they cost you the most in the long run. Prioritize paying off these high-interest debts first, while continuing to make minimum payments on the others.

- Develop a Repayment Strategy: There are two common strategies for debt repayment: the avalanche method and the snowball method. With the avalanche method, you focus on paying off the debt with the highest interest rate first, then move on to the next highest. The snowball method involves paying off the smallest debt first, then working your way up to larger debts. Choose the strategy that aligns with your financial goals and motivates you to stay on track.

- Increase Your Debt Payments: Allocate a larger portion of your income towards debt repayment. Look for areas in your budget where you can cut back on expenses to free up more funds for debt repayment. Consider taking on side gigs or part-time work to generate extra income that can be applied towards debt.

- Negotiate Lower Interest Rates: Contact your creditors and explore options for lowering your interest rates. In some cases, they may be willing to negotiate a lower rate, especially if you have a good payment history.

- Consolidate or Refinance Debt: If you have multiple high-interest debts, you may consider consolidating them into a single loan with a lower interest rate. Additionally, refinancing certain types of debt, such as student loans or mortgages, can help reduce interest rates and lower monthly payments.

Paying off debt requires discipline and perseverance. Stay committed to your repayment plan and track your progress along the way. If you find it challenging to manage your debts or need expert guidance, consider consulting with a financial advisor or credit counseling service.

By prioritizing the repayment of high-interest debts and actively working towards reducing liabilities, you can free up more money for savings and investments. This will ultimately accelerate your journey towards building wealth.

Furthermore, consider whether you have an emergency fund in place. Life is unpredictable; having a safety net can provide peace of mind during unexpected situations like job loss or medical emergencies.

Having an emergency fund is indeed essential for financial security. An emergency fund acts as a safety net to cover unforeseen expenses and provide peace of mind during challenging times. Here are some key points to consider:

- Determine Your Emergency Fund Goal: Calculate your monthly expenses and aim to save three to six months' worth of living expenses. This will provide you with sufficient funds to cover essential costs in case of emergencies.

- Start Saving Regularly: Set a budget and allocate a portion of your income towards your emergency fund. Treat it as a non-negotiable expense, just like paying your bills or mortgage. Consider automating your savings by setting up automatic transfers to your emergency fund account each month.

- Choose the Right Account: Keep your emergency fund in a separate account that is easily accessible but not easily spent. A high-yield savings account or a money market account can be good options, as they offer higher interest rates than regular savings accounts while still providing easy access to your funds when needed.

- Stay Focused and Consistent: Building an emergency fund takes time and discipline. Stay committed to your savings goal and avoid dipping into the fund for non-emergency expenses. If you do use the fund, replenish it as soon as possible.

- Adjust the Amount Based on Life Circumstances: As life circumstances change, reassess your emergency fund goal. For example, if you have dependents or work in an industry with less job security, you may want to save more to account for potential financial challenges.

- Reevaluate and Replenish: Periodically review your emergency fund to ensure it aligns with your current financial situation. If you've experienced an emergency and had to use the funds, make it a priority to replenish the amount as soon as possible.

An emergency fund is designed to provide financial stability during unexpected situations. By having one in place, you can better navigate unforeseen events without relying on credit cards or loans, which can lead to further debt. Start saving for your emergency fund today and enjoy the peace of mind it brings.

Assessing wealth isn't just about numbers on paper – it's also about mindset. How do you view money? Is it something that controls or empowers you?

Understanding the relationship between yourself and money plays a significant role in achieving financial success.

Your on money can indeed impact your financial success. Here are a few ways to view money that can shape your mindset:

- Money as a Tool: See money as a tool that you can utilize to achieve your goals and aspirations. By viewing money as a means to an end, you can focus on using it wisely and strategically to create the life you desire. This perspective empowers you to make informed financial decisions and leverage money to work for you.

- Money as a Resource: Recognize that money is a valuable resource that allows you to meet your needs, fulfill your desires, and support your loved ones. By viewing money as a resource, you can develop healthy habits such as budgeting, saving, and investing, which can lead to long-term financial stability and growth.

- Money as Freedom: Consider money as a source of freedom and independence. Financial security provides you with more choices and opportunities in life. With this mindset, you can strive for financial independence, allowing you to pursue your passions, take calculated risks, and make decisions based on what truly matters to you.

- Money as Energy Exchange: See money as an exchange of value for goods and services. This perspective encourages you to focus on delivering value to others through your work or business endeavors. By providing value, you can attract money and create a positive impact both financially and personally.

- Money as a Tool for Impact: View money as a means to make a positive difference in the world. When you have financial resources, you can contribute to causes you care about, support charitable organizations, or invest in sustainable and ethical projects. This perspective aligns your financial goals with your values and allows you to make a meaningful impact.

Remember, your mindset around money can influence your financial decisions and behaviors. By adopting a positive and empowering view of money, you can cultivate a healthy relationship with it and work towards achieving your long-term financial success.

In conclusion (as per instructions), taking stock of one's finances is an essential first step towards building lasting wealth. It allows us to pinpoint areas for improvement while highlighting our existing strengths. So gather those bank statements and start evaluating! The road to riches begins with an honest assessment of where you currently stand financially.

Taking stock of your finances is a crucial step in building lasting wealth. By evaluating your financial situation, you can identify areas for improvement and leverage your existing strengths. Here are a few key steps to start your financial assessment:

- Gather Financial Statements: Collect your bank statements, investment account statements, credit card statements, and any other relevant financial documents. This will give you a comprehensive overview of your current financial situation.

- Calculate Your Net Worth: Determine your net worth by subtracting your liabilities (debts) from your assets. This will give you a snapshot of your overall financial health and help you understand your wealth accumulation progress over time.

- Analyze Income and Expenses: Review your income sources and track your monthly expenses. This analysis will help you understand your cash flow and identify areas where you can potentially save or optimize your spending.

- Assess Debt Levels: Evaluate your outstanding debts, including credit card balances, loans, and mortgages. Determine the interest rates, minimum payments, and total amount owed for each debt. This assessment will allow you to prioritize debt repayment strategies and work towards becoming debt-free.

- Review Investment Performance: If you have investments such as stocks, bonds, or real estate properties, assess their performance. Determine if they align with your long-term financial goals and make adjustments if necessary.

- Evaluate Savings and Emergency Fund: Analyze your savings habits and determine if you have an emergency fund in place. Assess the adequacy of your savings and make adjustments to ensure you have a sufficient safety net for unexpected expenses.

- Set Financial Goals: Based on your financial assessment, establish short-term and long-term financial goals. These goals should be specific, measurable, attainable, relevant, and time-bound (SMART). They will serve as a roadmap for your financial journey.

Conducting a thorough financial assessment allows you to identify areas that need improvement and leverage your existing strengths. It provides a solid foundation for developing a financial plan and taking the necessary steps towards building lasting wealth.

Higher-Paying Jobs

When it comes to building wealth, one effective strategy is to pursue higher-paying jobs. By increasing your income, you can have more money available for saving and investing. Here are a few potential avenues to explore in your quest for a higher salary.

There are several avenues you can consider. Here are a few potential strategies to explore:

- Advance Your Education: Investing in your education can open doors to higher-paying job opportunities. Consider pursuing advanced degrees, certifications, or specialized training in your field of interest. This can enhance your skills and qualifications, making you a more competitive candidate for higher-paying positions.

- Acquire In-Demand Skills: Stay updated with the latest industry trends and identify high-demand skills that employers are seeking. Develop expertise in these areas through online courses, workshops, or on-the-job training. By acquiring valuable skills, you can position yourself for higher-paying roles within your industry.

- Seek Career Advancement: Look for opportunities to advance within your current organization. Take on additional responsibilities, seek promotions, or explore lateral moves that can lead to higher-paying positions. Demonstrate your value to the company by consistently delivering results and taking on leadership roles.

- Negotiate Salary: When applying for a new job or during performance reviews, don't be afraid to negotiate your salary. Research industry standards, know your worth, and articulate the value you bring to the organization. Negotiating your salary can significantly impact your earning potential.

- Explore Higher-Paying Industries: Consider industries that generally offer higher salaries. Research sectors that align with your interests and skills, and explore job opportunities within those industries. Industries such as technology, finance, healthcare, and engineering often have higher-paying positions available.

- Start Your Own Business: Entrepreneurship can provide opportunities for higher income potential. Identify a viable business idea, conduct market research, and develop a solid business plan. Starting your own business allows you to leverage your skills, passions, and expertise to create a potentially lucrative venture.

- Network and Build Relationships: Networking is an effective way to access job opportunities and increase your earning potential. Attend industry events, join professional organizations, and connect with professionals in your field. Building strong relationships can lead to valuable connections and job referrals.

Pursuing higher-paying jobs requires effort, continuous learning, and strategic planning. By investing in your skills, education, and networking, you can position yourself for higher earning potential and ultimately build wealth.

Consider upgrading your skills or education. In many industries, obtaining advanced degrees or certifications can lead to significant pay increases. Research the qualifications necessary for higher-paying positions in your field and make a plan to acquire them.

Additionally, staying informed about current job market trends can help you identify high-demand professions that offer lucrative salaries. Industries such as technology, healthcare, finance, and engineering often provide opportunities for well-compensated employment.

Another option is seeking out promotions within your current organization or looking for new job opportunities with better compensation packages. Networking and building strong professional relationships can be instrumental in uncovering these prospects.

Seeking promotions within your current organization or exploring new job opportunities can be a great way to increase your earning potential. Here are a few strategies to consider:

- Demonstrate Your Value: Show your dedication and commitment to your current role by consistently delivering excellent results. Take on additional responsibilities and showcase your skills and achievements. By demonstrating your value to the company, you increase your chances of being considered for promotions or salary increases.

- Seek Opportunities for Growth: Actively look for opportunities to expand your skill set and take on new challenges within your organization. This could involve taking on special projects, volunteering for cross-functional teams, or seeking out professional development opportunities. Showing a proactive attitude towards growth and development can make you a strong candidate for advancement.

- Build a Strong Professional Network: Networking is crucial for uncovering new job opportunities and accessing insider information about potential promotions. Attend industry events, join professional associations, and connect with colleagues and mentors in your field. Building strong relationships can lead to referrals and valuable connections that can help you advance in your career.

- Stay Updated on Industry Trends: Keep yourself informed about the latest trends and developments in your industry. Stay up-to-date with emerging technologies, market demand, and new job opportunities. This knowledge will enable you to position yourself strategically and pursue roles that offer better compensation packages.

- Polish Your Resume and Interview Skills: Ensure that your resume highlights your skills, achievements, and qualifications effectively. Tailor it to each job application to showcase how your experience aligns with the requirements of the role. Additionally, invest time in improving your interview skills to confidently articulate your value to potential employers.

- Explore External Job Opportunities: If you feel limited in your current organization, consider exploring job opportunities outside of it. Research companies known for offering competitive compensation packages in your industry. Utilize online job platforms, professional networks, and recruitment agencies to identify attractive positions that align with your career goals.

Seeking promotions or new job opportunities with better compensation packages requires proactive effort and strategic planning. By demonstrating your value, expanding your skills, building a strong network, and staying updated on industry trends, you increase your chances of finding higher-paying positions and advancing in your career.

Don't overlook the potential financial benefits of negotiating your salary during the hiring process or when discussing performance evaluations with employers. Demonstrating your value and highlighting your achievements can give you leverage in these negotiations.

Negotiating your salary can indeed have a significant impact on your financial well-being. Here are some tips to keep in mind when negotiating your salary:

- Do Your Research: Before entering salary negotiations, research the market value for similar roles in your industry and location. Websites like Glassdoor, Payscale, and LinkedIn Salary Insights can provide valuable salary data. This information will give you a realistic understanding of what to expect and help support your negotiation arguments.

- Highlight Your Value: During salary negotiations, emphasize the value you bring to the company. Discuss your accomplishments, skills, and experience that make you a strong candidate for the position. Clearly articulate how your contributions will benefit the organization and contribute to its success.

- Be Confident and Professional: Approach salary negotiations with confidence and professionalism. Practice your negotiation pitch beforehand to feel more prepared and self-assured. Maintain a respectful and positive attitude throughout the process, showcasing your professionalism to the employer.

- Consider the Full Package: Remember that salary is just one component of the overall compensation package. Take into account other factors such as benefits, bonuses, vacation time, flexible work arrangements, and professional development opportunities. These additional perks can enhance the overall value of the job offer.

- Be Flexible: While it's essential to know your worth, be open to negotiation and consider the employer's perspective as well. If the initial salary offer is not what you expected, propose alternative solutions such as performance-based raises or bonuses tied to specific goals. Finding a mutually beneficial agreement is key.

- Practice Active Listening: Pay attention to the employer's responses and engage in active listening during salary negotiations. Understand their concerns, interests, and constraints. This will help you tailor your negotiation strategy and find common ground that satisfies both parties.

- Consider Timing: Choose an appropriate time to discuss salary negotiations. It's often best to wait until you have received a formal job offer or during performance evaluations when you can demonstrate your value to the company. Timing your negotiation strategically can increase your chances of success.

Salary negotiations are a normal part of the hiring process. By doing your research, highlighting your value, and approaching negotiations with professionalism and confidence, you can increase your chances of securing a salary that reflects your worth and contributes to your financial well-being.

Pursuing a higher-paying job should align with both long-term career goals and personal interests. It's crucial to find fulfillment in what you do while also working towards financial prosperity.

Finding a higher-paying job should not only be about financial gain but also about aligning with your long-term career goals and personal interests. Here are a few considerations to keep in mind:

- Reflect on Your Values and Interests: Take time to assess your values, interests, and passions. What type of work excites you? What are your long-term career goals? Aligning your job search with your interests and values can lead to greater job satisfaction and fulfillment.

- Identify Growth Opportunities: Look for job opportunities that offer room for growth and advancement. Consider positions that will allow you to develop new skills, take on more responsibilities, and expand your knowledge in your field of interest. This will not only open doors to higher-paying positions but also provide personal and professional development.

- Seek Work-Life Balance: While pursuing a higher-paying job is important, don't overlook the importance of work-life balance. Consider factors such as flexible working hours, remote work options, and company culture to ensure that the job aligns with your desired lifestyle and personal well-being.

- Assess Long-Term Career Prospects: Research the long-term prospects of the industry and job role you are considering. Are there opportunities for growth and stability? Will the skills and experience gained in this position be valuable in the future job market? Considering these factors will help you make informed decisions about your career trajectory.

- Evaluate Job Satisfaction Factors: Along with financial considerations, evaluate other factors that contribute to job satisfaction. These may include work environment, company culture, professional relationships, and the impact of the work you will be doing. Finding fulfillment in your job is crucial for long-term happiness and success.

- Seek Mentorship and Guidance: Connect with professionals in your field who have achieved financial success while finding fulfillment in their careers. Seek mentorship and guidance from them to gain insights into the industry, career paths, and strategies for achieving both financial prosperity and personal fulfillment.

Pursuing a higher-paying job should not be solely driven by money. It's important to find a balance between financial goals and personal fulfillment. By aligning your career choices with your interests and values, seeking growth opportunities, and considering factors like work-life balance and job satisfaction, you can build a successful and fulfilling career.

Side Hustlers

Side hustles have become increasingly popular in recent years as individuals seek to boost their income and diversify their revenue streams. A side hustle refers to any additional job or gig that is pursued alongside a full-time job or main source of income. It provides an opportunity for individuals to leverage their skills, talents, and interests to generate extra money.

They offer flexibility and the ability to monetize skills and interests. Here are some benefits of having a side hustle:

- Additional Income: One of the primary reasons people pursue side hustles is to increase their income. Whether you want to pay off debts, save for a specific goal, or build a financial cushion, a side hustle can provide an extra stream of income.

- Skill Development: Side hustles often allow individuals to explore their passions and develop new skills. By pursuing work in areas of interest, you can enhance your knowledge, expertise, and versatility. This can be beneficial for personal growth and may even open up new career opportunities in the future.

- Diversification of Income: Relying solely on a single source of income can be risky. Having a side hustle diversifies your revenue streams, providing a safety net in case of job loss or economic downturns. It adds stability to your financial situation and reduces dependence on one source of income.

- Entrepreneurial Experience: Many side hustles involve running a small business or offering freelance services. This entrepreneurial experience can be valuable for learning about marketing, customer service, financial management, and other aspects of business ownership. It can also serve as a testing ground for potential full-time entrepreneurship.

- Pursuing Passions: Side hustles give you the opportunity to pursue your passions and turn them into income-generating activities. Whether it's photography, writing, graphic design, or any other talent or hobby, a side hustle allows you to monetize your skills and interests.

- Networking and Connections: Engaging in a side hustle can expand your professional network and provide opportunities for collaboration and partnerships. Building relationships in your chosen industry or niche can lead to new opportunities and connections that can benefit your career in the long run.

- Personal Satisfaction: Side hustles offer a sense of accomplishment and personal satisfaction. When you can earn money doing something you love or are passionate about, it can enhance your overall well-being and job satisfaction.

Managing a side hustle alongside a full-time job requires effective time management, discipline, and dedication. It's important to assess the feasibility of balancing both roles and ensure that your side hustle aligns with your long-term goals and values.

If you need inspiration or guidance on starting a side hustle, researching online resources, or attending workshops, can provide valuable insights.

One of the great advantages of side hustles is the flexibility they offer. Unlike traditional nine-to-five jobs, side hustles can be done on evenings and weekends, allowing individuals to pursue them at their own convenience. Additionally, side hustles often tap into passions or hobbies, which makes the work more enjoyable and fulfilling.

- Flexibility is a significant advantage of side hustles. Here are some key points about the flexibility and fulfillment that side hustles provide:

- Work on Your Own Schedule: Side hustles can be done outside of regular working hours, giving you the freedom to choose when and how much you want to work. This flexibility allows you to balance your side hustle with your main job, personal commitments, and other responsibilities.

- Pursue Your Passions: Side hustles often involve work that aligns with your passions, hobbies, or skills. This makes the work more enjoyable and fulfilling, as you are pursuing something you genuinely love and have a genuine interest in. It can provide a creative outlet and a sense of personal satisfaction.

- Explore New Interests: Side hustles can also be an opportunity to explore new interests and expand your horizons. You may discover talents or passions you didn't know you had, and use your side hustle as a platform for personal growth and self-discovery.

- Supplement Your Income: The additional income generated from a side hustle can make a significant impact on your financial situation. Whether you want to pay off debts, save for a specific goal, or simply have more disposable income, a side hustle can provide the financial boost you need.

- Build a Portfolio or Business: Side hustles can serve as a stepping stone for building a portfolio or even starting your own business. It allows you to gain experience, develop your skills, and establish a track record of success. This can be valuable when seeking future opportunities or transitioning to full-time entrepreneurship.

- Embrace Entrepreneurial Spirit: By pursuing a side hustle, you're embracing an entrepreneurial mindset. You take ownership of your work, make decisions, and manage your time and resources. This can enhance your problem-solving skills, creativity, and overall entrepreneurial abilities.

- Work-Life Balance: Side hustles can contribute to a healthier work-life balance. By having control over your schedule and pursuing work that you enjoy, you can reduce stress and create more harmony between your personal and professional life.

While side hustles offer flexibility and fulfillment, it's important to manage your time effectively and set realistic expectations. Prioritize self-care, set boundaries, and ensure that your side hustle doesn't detract from your main job or personal well-being.

There are numerous options when it comes to choosing a side hustle. Freelancing in fields such as writing, graphic design, web development, or photography has gained traction due to its potential for high earnings and remote work opportunities.

Other popular choices include starting an online store through platforms like Etsy or Shopify, offering consulting services based on expertise in a specific field, or even driving for ride-sharing companies like Uber or Lyft.

The key aspect of a successful side hustle is finding something that aligns with your skills and interests while also having market demand. By leveraging these factors effectively, you can maximize your earning potential from your side hustle.

In conclusion (never use "in conclusion"!), incorporating a well-thought-out side hustle into your financial strategy can significantly contribute to building wealth over time. Whether it's pursuing freelance projects during weekends or launching an online business after work hours - exploring new avenues outside of your regular job allows you to harness untapped sources of income while expanding your skillset along the way!

By incorporating a well-planned side hustle into your financial strategy, you can unlock additional income streams and build wealth over time. Here are some key points to remember:

- Diversifying Income: A side hustle provides an opportunity to diversify your sources of income, reducing reliance on a single paycheck. This can create a more stable financial foundation and provide a cushion in case of unexpected expenses or job loss.

- Wealth Building: Earning extra income through a side hustle allows you to allocate those funds towards building wealth. Whether it's saving for retirement, investing in stocks or real estate, or paying off debt, a side hustle can accelerate your progress towards your financial goals.

- Skill Development and Growth: Side hustles often involve pursuing work that aligns with your skills and interests. By investing time and effort into your side hustle, you can develop new skills and expand your knowledge, which can enhance your professional growth and open up new opportunities in the future.

- Flexibility and Autonomy: One of the great advantages of a side hustle is the flexibility it offers. You have control over your schedule and can choose projects or business ventures that align with your lifestyle and priorities. This autonomy can lead to a better work-life balance and increased job satisfaction.

- Entrepreneurial Mindset: Engaging in a side hustle nurtures an entrepreneurial mindset. You learn to think creatively, problem-solve, and take ownership of your work. These skills and mindset can be valuable not only in your side hustle but in other areas of your life and career as well.

- Unlocking Potential: A side hustle allows you to explore untapped potential and monetize your passions, hobbies, and talents. It's an opportunity to turn your skills and interests into a source of income, which can be personally fulfilling and rewarding.

Building a successful side hustle requires careful planning, dedication, and persistence. It's essential to assess market demand, set clear goals, and continuously adapt and refine your approach. By harnessing the power of a well-thought-out side hustle, you can create new pathways to financial growth and fulfillment.

4 Tips To Build Wealth

1. Venture Into Business

One effective way to build wealth is by venturing into your own business. Starting a business allows you to have control over your income and potential for growth. Whether it's a small online store or a large-scale enterprise, entrepreneurship offers endless possibilities.

Venturing into your own business can be a powerful means of building wealth and achieving financial success. Here are some key points to consider when starting a business:

- Control over Income: As a business owner, you have the ability to control your income. The success of your business directly impacts your earnings, allowing for unlimited potential for growth and profitability.

- Wealth Creation: Starting a business provides an opportunity to create wealth. By developing innovative products or services, targeting a specific market niche, and implementing effective strategies, you can generate substantial profits and build long-term wealth.

- Scalability and Growth: A successful business has the potential to scale and grow exponentially. With careful planning, strategic decision-making, and continuous adaptation, you can expand your operations, reach new customers, and increase your revenue streams.

- Flexibility and Autonomy: Entrepreneurship offers flexibility and autonomy that is often not found in traditional employment. You have the freedom to set your own schedule, make decisions, and pursue work that aligns with your passions and interests.

- Innovation and Creativity: Entrepreneurship encourages innovation and creativity. Starting a business allows you to bring new ideas to life, solve problems, and offer unique solutions to customers. This entrepreneurial mindset can fuel growth and competitive advantage in the market.

- Job Creation: As a business owner, you have the opportunity to create jobs and contribute to the economy. By hiring employees, you not only provide livelihoods but also make a positive impact on your community.

- Legacy and Long-Term Financial Security: Building a successful business can create a lasting legacy and provide long-term financial security for you and future generations. It allows you to establish assets and equity that can appreciate over time and provide ongoing income.

When starting a business, it's important to conduct thorough market research, develop a solid business plan, and seek guidance from mentors or professionals. Embrace a growth mindset, be prepared to face challenges, and continuously learn and adapt as you navigate the entrepreneurial journey.

Entrepreneurship requires dedication, perseverance, and a willingness to take calculated risks. However, with passion, hard work, and strategic decision-making, starting your own business can be a rewarding path to wealth creation and personal fulfillment.

One key aspect of venturing into business is identifying a profitable niche or market opportunity. Conduct thorough research to determine if there is demand for your product or service, and assess the competition in the industry. This will help you understand if there is room for growth and profitability.

Once you have identified a viable business idea, it's essential to create a comprehensive business plan. A solid plan will outline your goals, target market, marketing strategies, and financial projections. It will serve as a roadmap for your entrepreneurial journey and guide how to navigate potential obstacles.

Creating a comprehensive business plan is crucial for the success of your venture. Here are key elements to include in your business plan:

- Executive Summary: Provide an overview of your business idea, its mission, and your goals. This section should grab the reader's attention and summarize the key points of your plan.

- Company Description: Describe your company and its structure. Explain what products or services you offer and highlight your unique selling proposition that sets you apart from competitors.

- Market Analysis: Conduct thorough research on your target market, including customer demographics, preferences, and trends. Identify your target audience and analyze the competition to determine your competitive advantage.

- Product or Service Offering: Clearly outline your products or services, emphasizing their features, benefits, and value proposition. Explain how your offerings solve a problem or meet a need in the market.

- Marketing and Sales Strategy: Detail your marketing and sales tactics to reach your target audience and promote your products or services. Include information on pricing, distribution channels, and advertising strategies.

- Operations and Management: Outline the day-to-day operations of your business and the roles and responsibilities of key team members. Discuss any partnerships or collaborations that are essential to your operations.

- Financial Projections: Present financial forecasts, including sales projections, expenses, and profitability estimates. Include a cash flow statement, balance sheet, and income statement to demonstrate the financial viability of your business.

- Funding Request (if applicable): If you require external funding, clearly state your funding needs and provide a detailed explanation of how the funds will be used. Include a timeline for repayment if seeking a loan.

- Risk Assessment: Identify potential risks and challenges that your business may face. Develop contingency plans and mitigation strategies to address these risks effectively.

- Appendices: Include supporting documents such as market research data, resumes of key team members, product samples, or any other relevant materials.

A business plan is not a static document. It should be regularly reviewed and updated as your business evolves. It serves as a strategic tool to guide decision-making and secure financing if needed.

Securing adequate funding is another critical step when starting a new venture. Whether through personal savings, loans from family and friends, or seeking investors, having enough capital ensures that you can cover initial expenses such as equipment purchases, marketing campaigns, and hiring employees (if necessary).

Securing adequate funding is crucial for starting a new venture. Here are some common sources of funding to consider:

- Personal Savings: Using your own savings is a common way to fund your business. It allows you to retain full control and ownership while avoiding debt or equity obligations. However, it's important to assess the risk and ensure you have enough savings to cover initial expenses.

- Friends and Family: Borrowing from friends or family members can be an option if they believe in your business idea and are willing to provide financial support. However, it's crucial to approach this option with transparency and clear expectations to avoid straining personal relationships.

- Small Business Loans: Applying for a small business loan through banks or other financial institutions can provide the capital needed to start or expand your business. These loans typically require a solid business plan, collateral, and a good credit history.

- Crowdfunding: Platforms like Kickstarter and Indiegogo allow you to raise funds by pitching your business idea to a large online community. In return for their financial support, backers may receive rewards or pre-order products or services.

- Angel Investors: Angel investors are individuals or groups who provide funding to early-stage startups in exchange for equity or convertible debt. They often bring industry knowledge and connections along with their financial support.

- Venture Capitalists: Venture capitalists (VCs) invest in high-growth potential startups in exchange for equity. They typically invest larger amounts of capital and may also provide strategic guidance and mentorship.

- Grants and Government Programs: Research grants, loans, and government programs that are specifically designed to support small businesses. These can provide non-dilutive funding and resources to help you get started.

- Bootstrapping: Bootstrapping involves funding your business with minimal external resources and relying on your revenue to grow. While it requires careful financial management and slower growth initially, it allows for retaining full ownership and control.

When seeking funding, it's important to have a clear understanding of your financial needs, develop a compelling business plan, and be prepared to demonstrate the potential return on investment for potential investors or lenders. Furthermore, consider consulting with financial advisors or business mentors who can provide guidance on the best funding options for your specific situation.

Securing funding is just one aspect of starting a business. Effective financial management, cost control, and a sustainable revenue generation strategy are equally important factors in building a successful and profitable venture.

Building strong relationships with suppliers and customers is also crucial for long-term success in any business endeavor. Providing excellent customer service and delivering high-quality products or services are fundamental components of building trust with your target audience.

Building strong relationships with suppliers and customers is vital for the long-term success of any business. Here are some key points to consider:

● Supplier Relationships: Developing strong relationships with your suppliers is essential for ensuring a reliable and consistent supply chain. Open communication, trust, and mutual respect can lead to favorable terms, priority access to products or materials, and potential cost savings.

- Quality Products or Services: Providing high-quality products or services is crucial for building trust and loyalty among your customers. Consistently delivering on your promises and exceeding expectations will help establish a positive reputation and differentiate your business from competitors.

- Customer Service Excellence: Exceptional customer service is a cornerstone of building strong relationships with your customers. Promptly addressing inquiries or concerns, going the extra mile to solve problems, and maintaining clear and open lines of communication can foster trust and loyalty.

- Personalization and Customization: Tailoring your products or services to meet the specific needs and preferences of your customers can create a personalized experience that sets you apart. Understanding their pain points, preferences, and feedback can help you continuously improve and adapt your offerings.

- Feedback and Continuous Improvement: Actively seeking feedback from both suppliers and customers is crucial for understanding their needs and expectations. Regularly collecting and analyzing feedback can help identify areas for improvement and drive innovation in your business.

- Loyalty Programs and Incentives: Implementing loyalty programs or offering incentives can encourage repeat business and customer loyalty. Rewards, discounts, or exclusive offers can create a sense of appreciation and strengthen the relationship with your customers.

- Transparency and Integrity: Being transparent in your business practices, including pricing, policies, and product information, helps build trust and credibility. Operating with integrity and ethical standards fosters long-term relationships based on mutual respect and fairness.

- Effective Communication: Clear and effective communication is essential for fostering strong relationships with both suppliers and customers. Regularly update them on important information, such as product releases, changes in policies, or upcoming promotions.

Building relationships takes time and effort. Consistently delivering value, listening to feedback, and prioritizing customer satisfaction are key elements in establishing and maintaining strong relationships with both suppliers and customers.

Moreover, staying adaptable in an ever-changing marketplace is key - constantly monitoring industry trends helps ensure continued relevance while remaining open-minded about opportunities beyond what was initially planned.

In conclusion, venturing into entrepreneurship can be a rewarding path to building wealth. By combining careful planning, thorough research, securing adequate funding, developing strong relationships with suppliers and customers, and staying adaptable to market trends, you can increase your chances of success in the world of business. With determination, perseverance, and strategic decision-making, you have the potential to achieve financial prosperity and create a successful venture.

2. Increase Your Income

One effective way to build wealth is by increasing your income. While it may seem like a daunting task, there are several strategies you can implement to boost your earnings.

As mentioned previously, consider negotiating a higher salary or seeking out promotions at your current job. Showcasing your skills and proving your worth to employers can lead to higher wages and better opportunities for advancement.

Additionally, exploring additional streams of income through side gigs or freelance work can significantly increase your earning potential. Utilize your talents and passions outside of your regular job to generate extra cash flow.

Investing in yourself is another key aspect of increasing income. Continuously improving your skill set through professional development courses or certifications can make you more valuable in the job market, leading to higher-paying positions.

Furthermore, considering alternative career paths that offer higher salaries might be worth exploring. Research industries with high-demand jobs or niche markets where specialized skills are highly valued.

In conclusion, by focusing on increasing your income through negotiation tactics, diversifying revenue streams, investing in personal growth, and considering alternative career paths, you have the potential to significantly boost both short-term earnings and long-term wealth-building opportunities.

3. Improve Your Skill Set

Improving your skill set is a crucial step towards building wealth. By continuously learning and honing new skills, you open up opportunities for higher-paying jobs, promotions, and even the possibility of starting your own business. Here are some ways to improve your skillset and increase your earning potential.

Continuous learning and skill development are essential for increasing your earning potential and building wealth. Here are some ways to improve your skillset:

● Identify Key Skills: Assess the skills that are in demand in your industry or the field you want to pursue. Research job descriptions, industry trends, and talk to professionals to identify the key skills that can enhance your career prospects.

● Take Courses and Attend Workshops: Enroll in courses, workshops, or seminars that offer opportunities to learn new skills or enhance existing ones. Online platforms like Coursera,

Udemy, or LinkedIn Learning provide a wide range of courses taught by industry experts.

- Pursue Higher Education: Consider pursuing a degree or advanced certification in a field relevant to your career goals. Higher education can provide you with specialized knowledge and credentials that can set you apart from the competition.

- Seek Mentorship: Find mentors or industry professionals who can guide you and share their knowledge and experience. They can provide valuable insights, advice, and help you develop the skills necessary for success.

- Join Professional Associations: Become a member of professional associations or organizations related to your industry. These associations often offer resources, networking opportunities, and professional development programs to help you enhance your skills.

- Read Industry Publications and Books: Stay up-to-date with the latest trends, research, and best practices in your field by reading industry publications, blogs, and books. This will broaden your knowledge base and keep you informed about industry developments.

- Practice Continuous Learning: Make a habit of continuous learning by dedicating time each week to expand your knowledge. Listen to podcasts, watch educational videos, or read articles to stay informed about emerging trends and advancements in your industry.

- Embrace Technology: Develop proficiency in using technology and digital tools relevant to your field. Familiarize yourself with software programs, online platforms, or tools that can streamline processes and increase efficiency.

- Take on Challenging Projects: Seek out opportunities within your current job or volunteer for projects that allow you to develop new skills or stretch your existing abilities. Taking on challenging assignments can help you gain hands-on experience and showcase your capabilities to employers.

- Network and Collaborate: Engage with professionals in your field through networking events, industry conferences, or online communities. Collaborating with others can expose you to new ideas, perspectives, and skill sets.

Improving your skillset is an ongoing process. Stay motivated, embrace a growth mindset, and be proactive in seeking out learning opportunities. By continuously enhancing your skills, you can position yourself for career growth, higher earning potential, and ultimately, building long-term wealth.

Consider investing in education or professional development courses related to your field of interest. These programs can provide you with valuable knowledge and certifications that will make you stand out from the competition.

Seek out mentorship or coaching opportunities. Learning directly from someone who has already achieved success in your desired field can give you insights and guidance that can significantly accelerate your growth.

Seeking mentorship or coaching opportunities can be extremely valuable for your personal and professional growth. Here's why:

- Gain Real-World Insights: Mentors or coaches who have already achieved success in your desired field can provide you with valuable insights and real-world experiences. They can share their knowledge, lessons learned, and best practices, helping you avoid potential pitfalls and make informed decisions.

- Expand Your Network: Mentors and coaches often have extensive networks in your industry. By building a relationship with them, you can gain access to new connections, potential job opportunities, and referrals that can enhance your career prospects.

- Receive Personalized Guidance: A mentor or coach can provide personalized guidance tailored to your specific goals and challenges. They can help you identify areas for improvement, set meaningful objectives, and develop a roadmap for achieving success.

- Accelerate your Learning Curve: Learning from someone who has already achieved what you aspire to can significantly accelerate your learning curve. Mentors and coaches can provide you with shortcuts, strategies, and resources that can help you progress faster and more efficiently.

- Boost Your Confidence: Having a mentor or coach who believes in your abilities and provides guidance can boost your confidence. They can offer encouragement, support, and constructive feedback, which can help you overcome self-doubt and push through obstacles.

- Accountability and Motivation: Mentors and coaches can hold you accountable for your goals and provide motivation along the way. They can help you stay focused, track your progress, and provide the necessary push when you need it.

- Expand Your Skill Set: Mentors and coaches can help you identify and develop the skills necessary for success in your chosen field. They can suggest relevant training programs, recommend books or resources, and provide guidance on how to acquire the skills you need.

- Personal and Professional Growth: Mentorship or coaching goes beyond just acquiring knowledge and skills. It can also contribute to your personal growth by helping you develop important qualities such as resilience, adaptability, and leadership.

When seeking mentorship or coaching opportunities, consider reaching out to professionals in your industry, attending networking events, or joining mentorship programs offered by professional organizations. Be proactive in seeking guidance, and don't be afraid to ask for help.

Mentorship and coaching relationships are built on mutual respect and trust. Approach potential mentors or coaches with a clear understanding of what you hope to gain from the relationship and demonstrate your commitment to learning and growth.
By seeking out mentorship or coaching opportunities, you can tap into the wisdom and experience of others, accelerating your growth and increasing your chances of success in your desired field.

Additionally, don't be afraid to take on new challenges or projects at work. Volunteering for tasks outside of your comfort zone allows you to gain experience in different areas and expand your skill set organically.

Taking on new challenges and projects at work is an excellent way to expand your skill set and grow professionally. Here are a few reasons why you shouldn't be afraid to step out of your comfort zone:

● Skill Development: By volunteering for tasks outside of your comfort zone, you have the opportunity to develop new skills. These skills can be valuable assets that enhance your professional profile and open doors to new opportunities.

- Versatility: Being versatile and adaptable in the workplace is highly valued. Taking on diverse projects can help you become a well-rounded professional who can handle a variety of tasks and responsibilities.

- Increased Confidence: Successfully completing new challenges can boost your confidence and self-belief. It demonstrates your ability to take on unfamiliar tasks and excel, which can propel your career forward.

- Professional Growth: Embracing new challenges allows you to grow both personally and professionally. You'll learn from new experiences, gain insights from different perspectives, and develop problem-solving skills that can be applied in various situations.

- Expand Your Network: Engaging in new projects exposes you to different team members, departments, or even external stakeholders. This expands your professional network and creates opportunities for collaboration and future career growth.

- Recognition and Advancement: Taking on new challenges shows your willingness to go above and beyond your current role. It positions you as someone who is proactive, capable, and dedicated to personal and professional growth. This can lead to recognition, promotions, or new opportunities within your organization.

- Discover Hidden Talents: Stepping outside of your comfort zone may reveal hidden talents or passions that you were previously unaware of. Exploring new projects can help you uncover strengths and interests that can shape your future career path.

Taking on new challenges should be approached with enthusiasm and a growth mindset. Seek support and guidance from colleagues or mentors when needed, and don't be afraid to ask questions or seek additional training to ensure your success. Embrace the opportunity to learn and grow, and you'll reap the rewards in both personal and professional development.

Moreover, networking is essential for career growth. Attend industry events or join professional associations where you can meet like-minded individuals who may offer valuable advice or potential job opportunities.

Embrace lifelong learning by staying updated with trends and advancements in your industry through reading books, attending webinars or workshops, and subscribing to relevant newsletters or blogs.

Embracing lifelong learning is crucial for staying relevant and advancing in your career. Here are some ways to stay updated with trends and advancements in your industry:

- Read Books: Invest time in reading books written by industry experts or thought leaders. Look for books that cover current trends, emerging technologies, or best practices in your field. Reading allows you to gain in-depth knowledge and insights that can inform your work.

- Attend Webinars or Workshops: Participate in webinars or workshops related to your industry. These virtual or in-person events offer opportunities to learn from experts, gain practical skills, and stay up-to-date with the latest developments. Many organizations and professional associations host webinars and workshops on various topics.

- Subscribe to Newsletters and Blogs: Stay connected with industry news and updates by subscribing to relevant newsletters and blogs. These resources often provide valuable insights, case studies, and expert analysis that can broaden your understanding and keep you informed about industry trends.

- Follow Thought Leaders on Social Media: Identify thought leaders, influencers, and experts in your field and follow them on social media platforms like LinkedIn, Twitter, or industry-specific forums. Their posts, articles, and comments can provide valuable insights and keep you updated with the latest happenings in your industry.

- Join Online Communities: Participate in online communities or forums where professionals in your industry interact and share knowledge. Engaging in discussions, asking questions, and contributing to the community can expand your network and expose you to different perspectives and ideas.

- Engage in Continuous Professional Development: Take advantage of online platforms that offer professional development courses or certifications.

- Networking Events and Professional Associations: Attend industry conferences, networking events, or join professional associations related to your field. These events provide opportunities to connect with like-minded individuals, establish valuable relationships, and gain insights from industry leaders.

- Follow Industry News and Publications: Stay updated with industry news by subscribing to relevant publications or news outlets. This can include online magazines, trade journals, or newspapers that cover topics specific to your industry.

Lifelong learning is a continuous process. Make it a habit to set aside time for learning and staying updated with industry trends. By embracing lifelong learning, you'll position yourself as a knowledgeable professional and increase your chances of success in your career.

By continuously improving yourself professionally through expanding skills sets across various domains within an academic capacity while focusing on continuous self-improvement rather than summarizing it as a conclusive answer overall; one ensures they are consistently moving forward towards their financial goals without being repetitive about rehashing points previously mentioned.

Professional growth and continuous self-improvement are key to moving forward towards your financial goals. By expanding your skill sets across various domains and focusing on continuous learning, you ensure that you are consistently progressing in your career. This approach allows you to:

- Stay Relevant: The professional landscape is constantly evolving, and acquiring new skills keeps you up to date with the latest trends and advancements in your field. This ensures that you remain relevant and valuable in the job market.

- Enhance Your Marketability: By continuously improving yourself professionally, you enhance your marketability to potential employers or clients. A diverse skill set demonstrates versatility and adaptability, making you a desirable candidate for a wide range of opportunities.

- Open Up New Career Paths: Expanding your skill sets across various domains can open up new career paths and increase your earning potential. You may discover new interests and passions that lead you to explore different roles or industries.

- Improve Job Performance: Continuously improving yourself professionally allows you to enhance your job performance. As you acquire new skills and knowledge, you become more efficient, effective, and capable of taking on new challenges and responsibilities.

- Increase Confidence and Motivation: The process of continuous self-improvement boosts your confidence and motivation. As you achieve milestones and see tangible progress in your professional development, you gain a sense of accomplishment and the drive to keep pushing forward.

- Network Expansion: Engaging in continuous learning often involves connecting with other professionals, attending workshops, or joining industry-specific communities. These interactions provide opportunities to expand your network and build meaningful relationships with like-minded individuals.

● Adapt to Changing Industries: Industries go through cycles of disruption and transformation. By continuously improving yourself professionally, you develop the agility and resilience needed to adapt to changing industry dynamics and seize new opportunities.

Continuous self-improvement is a lifelong journey. It requires dedication, curiosity, and a growth mindset. Embrace new challenges, seek out learning opportunities, and stay proactive in your professional development. By doing so, you'll keep moving forward toward your financial goals and create a fulfilling and successful career path.

4. Create a Budget

Creating a budget is an essential step toward building wealth. By carefully tracking your income and expenses, you gain a clear understanding of where your money goes each month. This knowledge allows you to make informed decisions about how to allocate your resources and prioritize savings.
Here's why it's important and how it can help you achieve your financial goals:

- Understanding Your Financial Situation: By tracking your income and expenses, you gain a clear understanding of your financial situation. This includes knowing how much money you have coming in, where it's going, and what you can afford.

- Identifying Spending Habits: Budgeting helps you identify your spending habits and patterns. It allows you to see where your money is being allocated and whether there are areas where you can cut back or make adjustments to save more.

- Prioritizing Savings and Investments: A budget helps you prioritize saving and investing. By allocating a portion of your income toward savings and investments as part of your budget, you ensure that you are consistently setting aside money for future goals and building wealth.

- Setting Financial Goals: Budgeting enables you to set clear financial goals. Whether it's saving for a down payment on a house, paying off debt, or building an emergency fund, having a budget helps you establish these goals and track your progress toward achieving them.

- Controlling Spending and Avoiding Debt: With a budget, you have control over your spending. It helps you make conscious decisions about where and how you spend your money, reducing the likelihood of overspending and accumulating debt.

- Planning for Future Expenses: Budgeting allows you to plan for future expenses and avoid financial surprises. By accounting for irregular expenses like annual insurance premiums, vehicle maintenance, or vacations, you can set aside money in advance and avoid dipping into savings or relying on credit.

- Adapting to Changing Circumstances: A budget provides flexibility to adapt to changing circumstances. Whether it's a change in income, unexpected expenses, or new financial goals, having a budget allows you to make adjustments and stay on track.

- Building Wealth Over Time: By consistently tracking your income and expenses and making informed decisions about how to allocate your resources, a budget helps you build wealth over time. It allows you to save, invest, and grow your net worth.

To create a budget, start by tracking your income and expenses.

Categorize your expenses into necessities (e.g., housing, utilities, transportation) and discretionary spending (e.g., entertainment, dining out).

Identify areas where you can reduce expenses or find ways to increase your income.

Use budgeting tools or apps to make the process easier and more efficient.

Review and adjust your budget regularly to ensure it aligns with your financial goals and current circumstances. With consistent budgeting, you'll have a better understanding of your finances and be on your way to building wealth.

Here are some steps to help you effectively review and adjust your budget:

- Set a Regular Review Schedule: Establish a specific schedule for reviewing your budget. This could be monthly, quarterly, or any interval that works best for you. Consistency is key to staying on top of your finances.

- Gather Financial Information: Collect all relevant financial information, including income statements, bank statements, credit card statements, and any other financial documents.

This will provide a comprehensive overview of your current financial situation.

- Track Your Expenses: Review your expenses over the designated period. Categorize them into fixed expenses (e.g., rent/mortgage, utilities), variable expenses (e.g., groceries, entertainment), and discretionary expenses (e.g., dining out, vacations). Use budgeting software or apps to simplify this process.

- Compare Actual vs. Budgeted Amounts: Compare your actual spending with the budgeted amounts from the previous period. Identify any discrepancies or areas where you exceeded or fell short of your budgeted amounts.

- Analyze Spending Patterns: Look for patterns in your spending. Identify areas where you consistently overspend or areas where you can make adjustments to save more money. Consider both necessary expenses and discretionary spending.

- Evaluate Income Changes: If your income has changed since the last budget review, consider how it impacts your overall financial situation. Assess if you need to adjust your budget categories or allocate more money towards savings or debt repayment.

- Identify Financial Goals: Revisit your financial goals and assess whether they are still relevant and attainable. Adjust your budget to align with your current goals and prioritize accordingly. This may involve reallocating funds or setting new savings targets.

- Make Necessary Adjustments: Based on your analysis, make the necessary adjustments to your budget. Increase or decrease budgeted amounts for specific categories, cut back on discretionary spending if needed, and reallocate funds to align with your financial goals.

- Plan for Unexpected Expenses: Account for any upcoming or unexpected expenses that may affect your budget. Set aside funds in an emergency fund to cover these expenses without disrupting your overall financial plan.

- Monitor and Track Progress: After making adjustments to your budget, continue to monitor and track your progress regularly. Use budgeting tools or apps to help you stay on top of your finances and ensure that you are sticking to your revised budget.

To create an effective budget, start by gathering all relevant financial information, such as bank statements, bills, and pay stubs. Identify your sources of income and categorize your expenses into fixed (e.g., rent, utilities) and variable (e.g., groceries, entertainment). Use online tools or spreadsheets to calculate totals for each category.

Next, analyze the data to identify areas where you can reduce spending or reallocate funds toward saving and investing. Look for opportunities to trim unnecessary expenses or negotiate better deals on services like insurance or cable subscriptions.

Creating a budget is not just about restricting yourself; it's also about setting realistic goals and allowing yourself some room for enjoyment. Allocate funds for leisure activities or hobbies that bring you joy while still adhering to your overall financial plan.

Porven Ways To Make Money In 2022

In 2022, the world of money-making is ripe with opportunities waiting to be seized. One way to boost your income is by exploring the realm of freelancing. With the rise of remote work and digital platforms, freelancers are in high demand across various industries. Whether you're a skilled writer, graphic designer, or programmer, there's a niche for you to thrive in.

Freelancing has become an increasingly popular way to boost income and explore new opportunities. Here are some reasons why freelancing can be a great option for increasing your income:

- Flexibility and Work-Life Balance: Freelancing offers flexibility in terms of when and where you work. You can choose your own hours and set your own schedule, allowing for a better work-life balance.

- Diverse Income Streams: Freelancing allows you to diversify your income streams by working on multiple projects for different clients. This can provide stability and reduce reliance on a single source of income.

- Expanding Your Skillset: Freelancing provides an opportunity to expand your skillset and gain experience in new areas. As you take on different projects, you can learn and develop new skills that enhance your marketability.

- Greater Earning Potential: With freelancing, your earning potential is not limited by a traditional job salary. You have the opportunity to set your own rates, negotiate contracts, and take on additional projects to increase your income.

- Building a Portfolio and Network: Freelancing allows you to build a portfolio of work that showcases your skills and expertise. As you work with different clients, you also have the chance to expand your professional network, which can lead to more opportunities in the future.

- Independence and Autonomy: Freelancing gives you the freedom to be your own boss and make decisions independently. You have control over the type of projects you take on, the clients you work with, and the direction of your career.

- Remote Work Opportunities: The rise of remote work and digital platforms has made freelancing more accessible than ever. You can work from anywhere in the world as long as you have an internet connection, opening up a global pool of clients and opportunities.

- Pursuing Your Passions: Freelancing allows you to pursue your passions and work on projects that align with your interests. By choosing clients and projects that resonate with you, work becomes more fulfilling and enjoyable.

- To get started with freelancing, consider the following steps:

- Identify Your Skills and Niche: Determine your strengths and skills that are in demand in the freelance market. Find your niche and target industries or clients that align with your expertise.

- Build a Portfolio: Create a portfolio of your past work or projects to showcase your abilities. This can be in the form of a website, online profile, or samples of your work.

- Establish an Online Presence: Create professional profiles on freelancing platforms, social media, and professional networks to increase your visibility and connect with potential clients.

- Set Your Rates: Research industry standards and determine your rates based on your experience and the value you provide. Be open to negotiation but ensure that your rates align with your worth.

- Network and Market Yourself: Attend industry events, join online communities, and network with professionals in your field. Market yourself through online platforms, referrals, and word-of-mouth to attract clients.

- Deliver Quality Work and Meet Deadlines: Maintain professionalism and strive for excellence in your work. Meeting deadlines and exceeding client expectations will help you build a strong reputation and secure repeat business.

- Continuously Learn and Adapt: Stay updated with industry trends, technologies, and best practices. Invest in professional development to enhance your skills and stay competitive in the freelance market.

Remember, freelancing requires discipline, self-motivation, and effective time management. It may take time to establish yourself and build a steady client base, but with determination and dedication, freelancing can be a rewarding way to boost your income and explore new opportunities.

Another avenue worth exploring is investing in the stock market. While it may seem intimidating at first glance, with proper research and guidance, you can make your money work for you. Consider diversifying your portfolio by investing in stocks from different sectors to minimize risk.

Investing in the stock market can indeed be a great way to grow your wealth over time. Here are some key points to consider when exploring this avenue:

- Educate Yourself: Before diving into the stock market, take the time to educate yourself about how it works. Understand the basic concepts of investing, such as stocks, bonds, and mutual funds. Familiarize yourself with financial terms and learn how to analyze company performance.

- Set Clear Financial Goals: Define your financial goals and investment objectives. Determine whether you are looking for long-term growth, income generation, or a combination of both. Having clear goals will help guide your investment decisions.

- Develop a Diversified Portfolio: Diversification is crucial to managing risk in the stock market. Invest in stocks from different sectors, industries, and geographic regions. This helps spread out your investments and reduce the impact of any single stock's performance on your overall portfolio.

- Do Thorough Research: Conduct in-depth research on companies before investing in their stocks. Analyze their financial statements, earnings reports, competitive advantages, and future growth prospects. Use reputable sources like financial news websites, analyst reports, and company filings.

- Consider Risk Tolerance: Assess your risk tolerance and invest accordingly. Stocks can be volatile, and prices can fluctuate significantly. Make sure you are comfortable with the level of risk associated with your investments.

- Seek Professional Advice: If you're new to investing or feel overwhelmed, consider consulting with a financial advisor or broker. They can provide guidance tailored to your specific financial situation and help you make informed investment decisions.

- Practice Patience: Investing in the stock market is a long-term game. It's important to have a patient mindset and not get swayed by short-term market fluctuations. Stay focused on your long-term goals and avoid making impulsive decisions based on market volatility.

- Monitor Your Investments: Regularly review your investments and stay updated on market trends. However, avoid constantly checking stock prices, as this can lead to emotional decision-making. Instead, focus on the underlying fundamentals of the companies you have invested in.

- Consider Dollar-Cost Averaging: Rather than investing a lump sum, consider using a strategy called dollar-cost averaging. This involves investing a fixed amount of money at regular intervals, regardless of the market conditions. This strategy can help smooth out the impact of short-term market fluctuations.

- Stay Informed and Evolve: Keep learning and adapting as you gain experience in the stock market. Stay informed about market trends, economic indicators, and any changes that may impact your investments. Continuously educate yourself to make informed decisions.

However, investing in the stock market comes with risks, and past performance is not indicative of future results. It's important to do thorough research, diversify your portfolio, and make investment decisions based on your financial goals and risk tolerance.

Furthermore, if you have a flair for creativity and enjoy expressing yourself through visual mediums, consider starting an online business selling handmade crafts or artwork. Platforms like Etsy provide a global marketplace where individuals can turn their hobbies into profitable ventures.

Additionally, don't overlook the power of affiliate marketing. By partnering with reputable brands and leveraging your online presence (whether through blogging or social media), you can earn commissions when people purchase products through your unique affiliate links.

Affiliate marketing can be a lucrative way to generate income by promoting products or services online. Here's how you can get started with affiliate marketing:

Choose Your Niche: Select a niche that aligns with your interests, expertise, and target audience. This will help you build credibility and attract an engaged audience.

- Research Affiliate Programs: Look for reputable affiliate programs that offer products or services related to your niche. Consider factors such as commission rates, payment terms, and the quality of the products or services being offered.

- Build Your Online Presence: Establish a platform to promote your affiliate links. This can be a blog, website, YouTube channel, social media accounts, or a combination of these. Create high-quality content that provides value to your audience and integrates your affiliate links naturally.

- Select Relevant Products: Choose products or services that are relevant and valuable to your audience. Promote products that you have personally used or believe in, as this will increase trust and credibility.

- Disclose Your Affiliation: Be transparent with your audience by disclosing your affiliation with the brands or products you promote. This helps build trust and ensures compliance with legal regulations.

- Create Compelling Content: Develop engaging and informative content around the products or services you are promoting. This can include product reviews, tutorials, comparisons, or personal recommendations. Focus on providing value to your audience rather than solely promoting products.

- Drive Traffic: Employ various strategies to drive traffic to your content and affiliate links. This can include search engine optimization (SEO), social media marketing, email marketing, collaborations with other creators, or paid advertising.

- Track and Optimize: Monitor your affiliate marketing efforts and track the performance of your links. Analyze which strategies are driving the most conversions and optimize your approach accordingly. Experiment with different marketing techniques to find what works best for your audience.

- Stay Committed and Patient: Affiliate marketing takes time and effort to build momentum. Stay committed, consistently produce high-quality content, and be patient as you grow your audience and start generating income.

- Comply with Guidelines and Regulations: Familiarize yourself with the guidelines and regulations set by the affiliate programs and advertising platforms you use. Adhere to these guidelines to maintain a good relationship with the brands you partner with and avoid any potential issues.

Successful affiliate marketing requires building trust with your audience, providing valuable content, and selecting the right products or services to promote. Be transparent, authentic, and focus on delivering value to your audience, and the potential for earning commissions through affiliate marketing can be significant.

Lastly but certainly not least, consider tapping into the booming e-commerce industry by starting your own online store. With platforms like Shopify making it easier than ever before to set up shop digitally, selling physical or digital products has never been more accessible.

These are just a few proven ways that will help pave your path towards financial success in 2022! Remember that each opportunity requires dedication and effort on your part - but with determination and strategic thinking - there's no limit to what you can achieve on this financial journey! So go ahead and explore these avenues; who knows? This might just be the year when everything falls perfectly into place for you!

Promising Ways To Make Money In 2023 And 2024

The future holds endless possibilities for those seeking financial success. In the coming years of 2023 and 2024, there are several promising avenues that can lead you to make more money.
Here are some promising avenues to consider for making money in the years 2023 and 2024:

- E-commerce and Online Retail: The e-commerce industry is thriving and expected to continue growing. Starting an online store or expanding your existing online presence can be a lucrative opportunity. Platforms like Shopify, WooCommerce, and Amazon can help you reach a global customer base.

- Digital Products and Services: With the increasing demand for digital products and services, you can capitalize on this trend. Consider creating and selling e-books, online courses, software, graphic design services, digital marketing services, or freelance writing, among others.

- Subscription-Based Businesses: Subscription-based models, such as membership sites or subscription boxes, offer recurring revenue streams. Identify a niche market and create a valuable subscription-based offering that keeps customers engaged and coming back for more.

- Niche Blogging and Content Creation: Building a successful blog or content platform can generate income through various channels like affiliate marketing, sponsored content, advertising, and selling digital products. Choose a niche that aligns with your interests and expertise to attract a dedicated audience.

- Influencer Marketing: As social media continues to dominate, becoming an influencer in your niche can open doors to collaboration opportunities with brands. By cultivating a loyal following, you can monetize your influence through sponsored posts, brand partnerships, and product endorsements.

- Real Estate Investment: Investing in real estate has long been a proven wealth-building strategy. Look for emerging markets, rental properties, commercial real estate, or real estate investment trusts (REITs) to diversify your portfolio and generate passive income.

- Renewable Energy and Sustainable Investments: With the growing focus on environmental sustainability, investing in renewable energy sources like solar and wind power can be financially rewarding. Additionally, exploring sustainable businesses and green technologies can offer long-term growth potential.

- Freelancing and Remote Work: The gig economy continues to thrive, providing opportunities for freelancers and remote workers. Skills like web design, content writing, programming, digital marketing, and virtual assistance are in high demand. Platforms like Upwork and Freelancer can help you find clients and projects.

- Cryptocurrency and Blockchain Technology: The world of cryptocurrencies and blockchain technology presents both risks and rewards. Educate yourself about the market, stay updated on trends, and consider investing or trading in cryptocurrencies if you have a high-risk tolerance and understanding of the market dynamics.

- Health and Wellness Industry: The health and wellness industry is experiencing significant growth as people prioritize their well-being. Consider starting a health-focused business, offering fitness classes, wellness coaching, healthy meal planning, or developing and selling health-related products.

These are just a few potential avenues to explore. It's important to conduct thorough research, identify your strengths and interests, and adapt to the evolving market trends to increase your chances of success. Stay proactive, embrace opportunities, and be open to learning and adapting along the way.

The rise of digital currencies presents a lucrative opportunity. Investing in cryptocurrencies like Bitcoin or Ethereum has proven to be profitable for many individuals. With advancements in technology and increased acceptance of digital currencies, this trend is expected to continue growing.

Indeed, the rise of digital currencies, such as Bitcoin and Ethereum, has created significant opportunities for investors. Here are some key points to consider:

● Potential for High Returns: Cryptocurrencies have shown the potential for substantial returns on investment. Bitcoin, for example, experienced significant price appreciation over the years, making early investors wealthy.

- Diversification: Adding cryptocurrencies to your investment portfolio can provide diversification, as they have a low correlation with traditional assets like stocks and bonds. This can help reduce overall risk and potentially increase returns.

- Growing Acceptance: Digital currencies are gaining wider acceptance among individuals, businesses, and financial institutions worldwide. Major companies, including Tesla, PayPal, and Square, have started accepting cryptocurrencies as a form of payment. This increasing acceptance can drive further adoption and value appreciation.

- Technological Advancements: Blockchain technology, which underlies cryptocurrencies, has shown promise in revolutionizing various industries. As advancements continue, cryptocurrencies may find more use cases, further boosting their value and utility.

- Volatility and Risk: Cryptocurrencies are known for their volatility, with prices experiencing significant fluctuations in short periods. This volatility can present opportunities for traders but also carries higher risks. It's important to carefully analyze and understand the risks associated with cryptocurrency investments.

- Regulatory Landscape: The regulatory environment surrounding cryptocurrencies is evolving. Governments are developing frameworks to address concerns like money laundering, taxation, and consumer protection. Staying informed about the regulatory landscape is crucial for investors.

- Education and Research: Before investing in cryptocurrencies, it's essential to educate yourself about the technology, market dynamics, and potential risks. Stay updated on industry news, follow reputable sources, and consider consulting with financial advisors who specialize in cryptocurrencies.

- Long-Term Outlook: While cryptocurrencies have shown significant growth, their long-term future is still uncertain. Factors like market sentiment, technological advancements, regulatory developments, and competition can impact their value and adoption.

It's important to note that investing in cryptocurrencies carries inherent risks, and it's advisable to only invest what you can afford to lose. Consider your financial goals, risk tolerance, and consult with professionals before making investment decisions.

Another promising avenue lies within the realm of e-commerce. As online shopping continues to gain popularity, establishing your own online store can generate substantial income. Whether it's dropshipping products or creating your own unique brand, there are countless opportunities waiting to be explored.

E-commerce presents a promising avenue for generating income in today's digital landscape. Here are some key points to consider when starting your own online store:

- Choose a Profitable Niche: Research and identify a niche market that has demand and growth potential. Find a balance between your interests, target audience, and market trends to increase the likelihood of success.

- Select Your Business Model: Decide on a business model that suits your goals and resources. You can opt for dropshipping, where you sell products without holding inventory, or create and sell your own unique products. Other options include print-on-demand, affiliate marketing, or wholesale.

- Build Your Online Store: Utilize e-commerce platforms like Shopify, WooCommerce, or BigCommerce to set up your online store. These platforms provide user-friendly interfaces, customizable design templates, and secure payment gateways to streamline the buying process.

- Source Products: If you choose dropshipping, research and partner with reliable suppliers who can fulfill orders on your behalf. If you plan to sell your own products, find manufacturers or establish a production process to ensure quality and timely delivery.

- Develop a Marketing Strategy: Create a comprehensive marketing plan to attract customers to your online store. Utilize social media marketing, content marketing, search engine optimization (SEO), paid advertising, influencer collaborations, and email marketing to drive traffic and conversions.

- Optimize User Experience: Focus on providing a seamless and user-friendly experience for your customers. Make sure your website is mobile-responsive, easy to navigate, and optimized for fast loading speeds. Offer secure payment options and provide excellent customer service to build trust and loyalty.

- Implement Effective SEO Strategies: Implement SEO techniques to improve your store's visibility in search engine results. Conduct keyword research, optimize product descriptions and titles, and build quality backlinks to enhance your search rankings and attract organic traffic.

- Leverage Social Media: Utilize social media platforms to build brand awareness, engage with your target audience, and drive traffic to your online store. Create compelling content, run targeted ads, and collaborate with influencers to expand your reach.

- Monitor and Analyze Performance: Regularly track and analyze key metrics such as website traffic, conversion rates, customer retention, and average order value. Use this data to identify areas for improvement and make data-driven decisions to optimize your store's performance.

- Stay Updated and Evolve: The e-commerce landscape is constantly evolving, so it's essential to stay updated on industry trends, consumer behavior, and emerging technologies. Adapt your strategies, experiment with new ideas, and continuously improve to stay competitive in the market.

Building a successful online store requires time, effort, and dedication. It's important to provide value, differentiate yourself from competitors, and consistently deliver an exceptional customer experience.

Additionally, with the increasing focus on sustainability and eco-friendly practices, green businesses are set to thrive in the coming years. From renewable energy solutions to eco-conscious consumer products, tapping into this market can not only make you financially successful but also contribute positively towards a better future.

The focus on sustainability and eco-friendly practices presents a great opportunity for green businesses to thrive. Here are some areas within the green sector that hold promise:

- Renewable Energy: As the world transitions towards cleaner and more sustainable energy sources, investing in renewable energy solutions like solar, wind, and hydroelectric power can be financially rewarding. This includes developing renewable energy projects, installing solar panels, or providing energy-efficient solutions.

- Sustainable Agriculture: With increasing consumer demand for organic and locally sourced food, sustainable agriculture practices are gaining popularity. Consider starting an organic farm, vertical gardening, or offering sustainable farming solutions like aquaponics or hydroponics.

- Eco-friendly Products: Designing and selling eco-friendly products can cater to the growing consumer preference for sustainable options. This includes products made from recycled materials, biodegradable packaging, sustainable fashion, zero-waste lifestyle products, or natural and organic personal care items.

- Green Building and Construction: The construction industry is embracing sustainable building practices. Offering green building services, energy-efficient home designs, or eco-friendly construction materials can be lucrative in this market.

- Waste Management and Recycling: With the increasing focus on waste reduction and recycling, starting a waste management or recycling business can be profitable. This includes recycling electronics, plastic, paper, or offering composting services.

- Sustainable Transportation: As the need for eco-friendly transportation options grows, consider entering the market with electric vehicle charging stations, bike-sharing programs, or promoting carpooling and ride-sharing services.

- Water Conservation and Treatment: With water scarcity becoming a global concern, businesses that offer water conservation solutions or water treatment technologies can thrive. This includes rainwater harvesting systems, water-efficient irrigation solutions, or water filtration systems.

- Environmental Consulting: Providing environmental consulting services to businesses and individuals can help them adopt sustainability practices and comply with regulations. This includes conducting environmental impact assessments, offering energy audits, or providing green certifications.

- Eco-tourism and Sustainable Travel: With the rise of conscious travelers, eco-tourism and sustainable travel businesses can flourish. This includes offering eco-friendly accommodations, organizing nature-based tours, or promoting responsible travel practices.

- Education and Awareness: Educating and raising awareness about environmental issues and sustainable practices can be a rewarding venture. This can involve offering sustainability workshops, creating educational content, or conducting awareness campaigns.

Remember to research your chosen green business sector thoroughly, identify target markets, and develop a compelling value proposition. Stay updated on industry trends, regulations, and customer preferences to remain competitive in this growing market.

Lastly yet importantly is the gig economy which shows no signs of slowing down. Freelancing platforms offer various gigs catering to diverse skills such as graphic design, content writing, web development – allowing individuals flexibility while earning a handsome income.

In conclusion, the next few years present immense potential for wealth creation through avenues like digital currency investments, e-commerce ventures, green businesses, technology-related jobs and participation in the gig economy.
Keeping an eye on emerging trends and adapting accordingly will give you an edge over others who may miss out on these promising opportunities.

How You Can Get Rich

So, you want to know how you can get rich. Well, let me tell you, it's not as easy as snapping your fingers and poof! Suddenly, money is raining down on you. No, my friend, getting rich takes hard work, dedication, and a strategic mindset.

Getting rich is not an overnight process, but rather a journey that requires effort and strategic thinking. Here are some key principles to keep in mind:

● Set Clear Goals: Define your financial goals and create a roadmap to achieve them. Having specific and achievable targets will help guide your actions and motivate you along the way.

- Develop Multiple Streams of Income: Relying solely on one source of income can be risky. Explore opportunities to diversify your income by investing in stocks, real estate, starting a side business, or engaging in passive income streams like affiliate marketing or rental properties.

- Invest Wisely: Educate yourself about different investment options such as stocks, bonds, mutual funds, and real estate. Consider working with a financial advisor to create an investment strategy tailored to your risk tolerance and long-term goals.

- Prioritize Saving and Budgeting: Cultivate a habit of saving a portion of your income regularly. Create a budget to track your expenses and identify areas where you can cut costs. Saving and budgeting will provide you with the foundation for building wealth.

- Continuously Learn and Improve: Stay updated on industry trends, market changes, and emerging opportunities. Invest in your knowledge and skills through courses, workshops, or networking events. Being adaptable and continuously learning will give you a competitive edge.

- Embrace a Growth Mindset: Believe in your ability to learn and grow. Be open to taking calculated risks and view failures as learning experiences. Embrace challenges and persist through setbacks on your path to success.

- Surround Yourself with the Right People: Build a network of supportive and like-minded individuals who share your aspirations. Connect with mentors, join professional organizations, or participate in online communities to gain insights and guidance from those who have achieved financial success.

- Be Disciplined and Patient: Building wealth takes time, so be patient and stay disciplined. Avoid impulsive decisions and stick to your long-term financial plan. Delayed gratification and staying focused on your goals will yield better results in the long run.

- Give Back and Practice Gratitude: As you accumulate wealth, remember to give back to your community and those in need. Practicing gratitude for what you have fosters a positive mindset and attracts more abundance into your life.

- Maintain a Healthy Work-Life Balance: While it's important to work hard towards your financial goals, don't neglect your well-being and relationships. Strive for a healthy work-life balance to avoid burnout and enjoy the journey to wealth.

The journey to getting rich is personal, and everyone's path may vary. It's crucial to define what wealth means to you beyond just monetary success and align your actions with your values.

One of the most important things you need to do is invest wisely. Whether it's in stocks or real estate, putting your money into assets that have the potential for growth is key. But remember to do thorough research before diving in headfirst!

Another way to increase your wealth is by starting your own business. Being an entrepreneur allows you to take control of your financial destiny. It may require long hours and sleepless nights initially but with perseverance and determination success will follow.

Starting your own business can be a rewarding way to increase your wealth and gain financial independence. Here are some key points to consider when starting a business:

- Identify a Profitable Niche: Research and identify a market gap or demand that aligns with your skills, expertise, and passion. Choose a niche where you can offer unique value to customers and have the potential for growth.

- Develop a Solid Business Plan: Create a comprehensive business plan that outlines your goals, target market, marketing strategies, financial projections, and operational details. A well-crafted business plan will guide your decision-making and attract investors if needed.

- Secure Adequate Funding: Determine the financial resources required to start and sustain your business. Explore different funding options such as personal savings, loans, grants, or seeking investments from angel investors or venture capitalists.

- Build a Strong Team: Surround yourself with a talented and dedicated team that shares your vision and can contribute to the success of your business. Hire individuals with complementary skills and expertise to fill key positions.

- Focus on Customer Acquisition and Retention: Develop effective marketing strategies to attract and retain customers. Understand your target audience, build brand awareness through advertising, social media, and networking, and provide excellent customer service to create loyal customers.

- Embrace Innovation and Adaptability: Stay updated on industry trends and embrace innovation in your products, services, or processes. Be open to feedback, adapt quickly to changing market dynamics, and continuously improve your offerings to stay competitive.

- Manage Finances Effectively: Establish sound financial management practices to ensure the sustainability of your business. Monitor cash flow, budget wisely, and keep track of expenses and revenue. Consider working with an accountant or financial advisor to make informed financial decisions.

- Foster a Strong Work Ethic and Resilience: Being an entrepreneur requires dedication, hard work, and resilience. Be prepared to put in long hours, face challenges, and overcome obstacles along the way. Stay motivated and focused on your long-term goals.

- Seek Mentorship and Networking Opportunities: Connect with experienced entrepreneurs, join industry associations, and seek mentorship from successful business leaders. Learn from their experiences, gain valuable insights, and expand your network for potential partnerships or collaborations.

- Continuously Learn and Improve: Stay curious and committed to learning and self-improvement. Attend workshops, seminars, and conferences related to your industry. Invest in your own personal and professional development to stay ahead in the competitive business landscape.

Entrepreneurship comes with its own risks and rewards. Be prepared for the journey and don't be discouraged by setbacks. With perseverance, determination, and a strategic approach, starting your own business can lead to financial success and personal fulfillment.

Additionally, don't be afraid to take calculated risks. Sometimes stepping outside of your comfort zone can lead to big rewards. However always make sure that these risks are well thought out and aligned with your goals.

Taking calculated risks can open up new opportunities for growth and financial success.

If you want to improve your capibility of decision taking I recommand *''TAKE DECISIONS!: Be Decisive Learn How to Make Tough Decisions Quickly''* by Barret Phoenix

Anyway here are some key points to consider when taking risks:

- Evaluate the Potential Rewards: Before taking a risk, assess the potential rewards it can bring. Consider the potential financial gains, personal growth, or advancement towards your goals. Ensure that the potential benefits outweigh the potential drawbacks.

- Conduct Thorough Research: Gather as much information as possible about the risk you're considering. Analyze market trends, conduct market research, and seek advice from experts or mentors who have experience in that area. Having a solid understanding of the risks involved will help you make informed decisions.

- Assess Your Risk Tolerance: Understand your own risk tolerance and comfort level. Some individuals are more inclined to take higher risks, while others prefer a more conservative approach. Find a balance that aligns with your personality and long-term goals.

- Plan for Contingencies: Anticipate potential challenges or setbacks and have contingency plans in place. Identify alternative paths or solutions to mitigate the impact of any negative outcomes. Being prepared can help minimize potential losses and keep you on track towards your goals.

- Start Small and Scale Gradually: If you're venturing into a new business or investment opportunity, consider starting small and gradually scaling up as you gain more experience and confidence. This allows you to test the waters and adjust your strategy if needed before committing significant resources.

- Learn from Failure: Understand that not every risk will lead to success. Failure is a natural part of the journey, and it's important to learn from your mistakes and setbacks. Use them as valuable learning experiences to refine your approach and make better decisions in the future.

- Trust Your Instincts: While thorough research and analysis are crucial, don't ignore your intuition and gut feelings. Sometimes, a well-informed gut instinct can guide you towards the right decision. Trust yourself and your ability to make sound judgments.

- Seek Advice and Support: Reach out to mentors, advisors, or peers who can provide guidance and support. Their insights and experiences can help you assess the risks more effectively and provide valuable perspectives.

- Maintain a Long-Term Perspective: When taking risks, it's important to focus on the long-term picture. Evaluate the potential impact on your overall goals and consider how the risk aligns with your broader vision. Short-term setbacks should not deter you from pursuing opportunities that have the potential for long-term success.

- Stay Flexible and Agile: Be adaptable and willing to adjust your strategy as new information or circumstances arise. The ability to pivot and make necessary changes can help you navigate risks more effectively and increase your chances of success.

Calculated risks can lead to great rewards, but it's essential to approach them with careful consideration and a clear understanding of the potential outcomes. By staying informed, being prepared, and trusting your judgment, you can take calculated risks that align with your goals and increase your chances of achieving financial success.

Furthermore,don't forget about the power of education.

Being knowledgeable about personal finance strategies such as budgeting,saving,and investing can go a long way in building wealth.

Education plays a crucial role in building wealth and financial success. Here are some ways education can empower you to make informed financial decisions:

- Personal Finance Education: Educate yourself on personal finance strategies such as budgeting, saving, and investing. Understand the principles of managing money effectively, creating a budget that aligns with your goals, and implementing strategies to save and invest wisely.

- Financial Literacy: Develop financial literacy by learning about different financial products, terms, and concepts. Understand how interest rates work, the benefits of compound interest, the importance of credit scores, and how to manage debt responsibly. This knowledge will help you make sound financial decisions and avoid common pitfalls.

- Investment Education: Gain knowledge about different investment options, such as stocks, bonds, mutual funds, real estate, or other alternative investments. Understand the risks and potential returns associated with each asset class and develop an investment strategy that aligns with your risk tolerance and goals.

- Continuous Learning: Stay updated on current financial trends, market fluctuations, and new investment opportunities. Read financial books, attend seminars or webinars, follow reputable financial blogs or podcasts, and consider taking courses on personal finance or investing. The more you learn, the better equipped you'll be to navigate the financial landscape.

- Seek Professional Advice: Consider working with a financial advisor who can provide personalized guidance based on your specific financial situation and goals. A qualified advisor can help you create a comprehensive financial plan, identify investment opportunities, and provide ongoing support and advice.

- Learn from Successful Individuals: Study the habits and strategies of successful individuals who have achieved financial success. Read biographies or listen to interviews of entrepreneurs, investors, and financial experts to understand their mindset, approaches, and lessons learned. Their experiences can provide valuable insights and inspiration.

- Teach Financial Literacy: Share your knowledge and educate others about personal finance. Teach your children or family members about money management, budgeting, and the importance of saving. Consider volunteering or getting involved in initiatives that promote financial literacy in your community.

Remember, education is a lifelong journey, and continuously expanding your financial knowledge will empower you to make well-informed decisions that can lead to wealth creation and financial independence.

Lastly,but not least,live below your means.

This doesn't mean living like a pauper,but rather being mindful of unnecessary expenses so that more money can be saved or invested for future growth.

It's all about making smart choices with every dollar earned.

In conclusion, getting rich takes time,discipline,and patience.

There are no shortcuts or instant fixes.

But by following these principles,you'll be setting yourself up for financial success.

So go ahead,take charge of yout finances,start taking action today,and watch yourself grow richer year after year!

Conclusion

In this book, we have explored proven ways to make money in 2022, as well as promising opportunities for the years ahead. We have discussed various strategies and ideas that can help you increase your income and achieve financial success.

It is important to remember that making more money requires effort, dedication, and sometimes taking calculated risks. There is no magic formula or shortcut to becoming rich overnight. However, by implementing the right strategies and having a solid plan in place, you can significantly improve your financial situation over time.

Whether it's starting a side hustle, investing in stocks or real estate, leveraging your skills through freelancing or online businesses – there are countless possibilities available for you to explore. The key is to find what aligns with your interests and strengths while also considering market trends and demands.

Remember to continuously educate yourself about personal finance, investment opportunities, and emerging industries. Stay informed about new technologies that could revolutionize certain markets or create new ones altogether. Adaptability is crucial in today's ever-changing world.

Don't forget the importance of patience and perseverance. Building wealth takes time; it seldom happens overnight. Set realistic goals for yourself along the way so that you can measure progress and celebrate milestones achieved on your journey towards financial freedom.

So go ahead - take action! Start implementing some of these ideas into your life today! With determination coupled with smart decision-making based on sound research and analysis – there's no limit to what you can achieve!

www.ingramcontent.com/pod-product-compliance
Lightning Source LLC
Chambersburg PA
CBHW072317290526
45794CB00002B/699